Twenty to

Simple
Statement
Rings

Carolyn Schulz

Search Press

First published in 2015

Search Press Limited
Wellwood, North Farm Road,
Tunbridge Wells, Kent TN2 3DR

Text copyright © Carolyn Schulz 2015

Photographs by Fiona Murray

Photographs and design copyright
© Search Press Ltd 2015

Print ISBN: 978-1-78221-257-7
EPUB ISBN: 978-1-78126-302-0

Suppliers
If you have difficulty in obtaining any of the
materials and equipment mentioned in this book,
then please visit the Search Press website for
details of suppliers: www.searchpress.com

Printed in China

Dedication

*I dedicate this book to my aunties, Lois Foley and
Inez Wright. Your encouragement and support are so
appreciated and I love you both dearly!*

Contents

Introduction 4

Materials and tools 6

Techniques and tips 7

Alternating Bead Ring 8

Focus Ring 10

Vintage-style Ring 12

Double-stranded Ring 14

Diamante Spacer Bar Ring 16

Fancy Spacer Bar Ring 18

Lavish Cha-cha Ring 20

Precious Flower Ring 22

Duet Ring 24

Fabulous Cluster Ring 26

Extravagant Cluster Ring 28

Solitaire Ring 30

Fancy Solitaire Ring 32

Swirled Multi-strand Ring 34

Beaded Ring with Coils 36

Chain Stitch Beaded Ring 38

Flat-stitched Lacy Ring 40

Right-angle Weave Band 42

Right-angle Weave Focus 44

Ring of Daisies 46

Introduction

Over the twenty years that I have been teaching jewellery, making rings has become one of my favourite projects. My students love the stunning results they can achieve in a short space of time with a minimum of investment. Many have also found rings are not just quick to make, but also easy to sell.

When the whole concept of a *Twenty to Make* book on rings started to form in my mind, I wanted to pull together not just techniques that were fun and easy to use, but rings that were fun and easy to wear! As I got stuck into the project I was delighted with the burst of creative ideas that flooded my mind (and my studio). Instead of twenty to make, I had more than a hundred rings to choose from!

Within these pages I am covering my three favourite ring-making techniques: stretchy cord, weaving and working with wire. I am so excited by the beautiful, sophisticated rings that can be created on stretchy cord. They are easy to make, comfortable to wear and eliminate that syndrome of 'ring twisting' where the main focus of the ring is always rotating to the back or side of the finger. Although woven rings take slightly more time, I find the creative process particularly therapeutic (I am told this is due to the bi-lateral hand and eye coordination). Working with wire is just plain 'wild' – you never know exactly how it will turn out and each creation is uniquely exquisite.

'Statement rings' is quite a claim, and yet I have found that even the most subtle simplicity can make a statement. I hope these rings will inspire you, whether you are a total beginner or an experienced jewellery artist. I will just add this warning… making jewellery, rings in particular, can be addictive!

Materials and tools

Materials:

Stretchy cord This elasticated cord is used for threading the beads onto for perfect-fit stretchy rings.

WildFire thread is thermally bonded thread that cannot be pierced with a needle. It is very strong yet supple, waterproof, can be knotted with zero stretch and will not fray.

Clear nail polish is useful to paint onto knots in stretchy cord to secure them.

Freshwater pearls can be used as focal beads.

Bicone crystals are faceted glass beads shaped like two faceted cones joined together at their base.

Daisy spacer beads These decorative flat spacer beads are in the shape of a daisy (sometimes called snowflake spacers).

Diamante spacer beads look like tyre hubcaps with diamante stones decorating the rim. They are used between beads to add interest and sparkle.

Seed beads These small beads are often used for weaving jewellery designs, for stringing or as spacer beads. Popular sizes range from 15/0 (smaller) to 6/0 (larger).

Crystal rondelles are faceted crystals that are not quite spherical, but short and wide.

Bead caps These decorative metal components are used to frame or enhance beads.

0.8mm wire is silver-plated and used for making wire-wrapped rings.

Ball end head pin This is a length of wire with a round ball end, which inconspicuously holds a bead while a loop is formed above it. It is used to attach beads to a jewellery piece.

Tools:

Round-nose pliers Both jaws are round, tapered cones and are used for creating loops as well as bending and shaping wire. Most commonly used to create loops on head pins and eye pins. **Chain-nose pliers** have flat jaws inside and are rounded on the outside. Ensure that the inside of the jaws are smooth, as ridged or textured jaws will mar the wire. They are used to grip components, bend wire, crimp, and so on. **Nylon-jaw pliers** are used to smooth out the wire if it gets bent or kinked at any point.

Ring mandrel This tool has markings on it to indicate different ring sizes. It will help ensure that your ring starts out, and stays, the size you want it to be when finished. It will also ensure that the ring stays round, so it will be comfortable to wear.

Scissors are useful for cutting elastic thread.

Wire cutters are used to cut jewellery wire.

Split-eye needle This type of needle is ideal for stringing lots of beads as it has a very large eye.

Techniques and tips

How to make a double surgeon's knot

1 Cross the left end of the cord over the right end, and bring it round twice, then pull.

2 Cross the right end of the cord over the left end of the cord and bring it round twice, then pull.

3 Now pull all four strands that are coming out of the knot tightly until it catches (pull the two on the left to the left, and the two on the right to the right).

4 Glue the knot to seal and secure it.

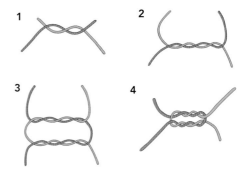

How to make a daisy chain

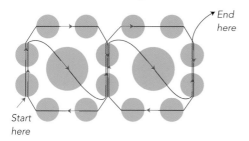

Start here

End here

1 Thread 8 beads onto some WildFire thread (or 12 beads, depending on the size of daisy desired – see page 46 for instructions using 12 beads).

2 Pass the cord back through the first two beads from step 1, going in the same direction, to form a circle.

3 Add a centre bead and pass through bead 6, then bead 5, from step 1. This will be going in the opposite direction from the circle formed in step 2.

4 For the next daisy, add 6 beads to the cord. Pass the cord back through bead 6, then bead 5, from step 1 and 3 (and in the same direction as step 3), forming a circle.

5 Add a centre bead and pass the cord through bead 4, then bead 3 from step 4, going in the opposite direction from the circle formed in step 4.

Ring types explained

Perfect-fit Stretchy Rings (pages 8–21)

Rings made on stretchy cord can be made to fit your finger size perfectly so that they stay put when you wear them. With the stretch, they easily pass over knuckles that are larger.

Wire-wrapped Rings (pages 22–37)

These rings are both quick and easy to make with a little practice, and can look very professional and stylish.

Woven Rings (pages 38–47)

These gorgeous rings are created by weaving beads in delicate patterns using a split-eye needle. They are made with seed beads and combinations of pearls and crystals.

Safety tips when working with wire:

- The use of safety glasses is always recommended.
- Always hold both ends of the wire being cut. If you cannot hold both, hold the wire in such a way that the loose end will not become a potential hazard (put a hand or finger over where you are cutting, cut under a beading mat or cut inside a bag).
- Use cutters and all tools with care.

Alternating Bead Ring

Materials:

Approx. 10–12 x 3 x 4mm faceted rondelles in amber and taupe

Stretchy cord

Clear nail polish

Tools:

Scissors

Split-eye needle

Instructions:

1 Working from the reel or a long strand of cord (this makes it more economical), thread about 2–3cm (¾–1¼in) of cord through the split-eye needle.

2 Thread the beads onto the cord, alternating opaque and transparent. The number of beads used will be determined by the size of ring required.

3 Remove the needle, cut the cord at the required length and tie the two cord ends together using a double surgeon's knot (see page 7).

4 Pull the beads aside to expose the knot. Tug gently until the knot catches.

5 Re-thread the shorter tail through the needle and pass it through the closest bead (do not pull the knot into the bead yet). Then remove the needle.

6 Coat the knot with clear nail polish to seal and secure.

7 Tug gently on the short tail until the knot pops into the bead.

8 Allow the nail polish to dry. Pull each cord gently away from the bead, taking care not to pull the knot back out of the bead, and snip the excess cord.

Alternating transparent and opaque beads in coordinating colours adds interest and sparkle to the most basic of ring bands. For a different effect, use jade and orange beads (see above).

Focus Ring

Materials:
Approx. 18–20 x 3mm black glass pearl beads
1 x 4 x 6mm faceted black oat bead
2 x 2.4mm metal spacer beads
Stretchy cord
Clear nail polish

Tools:
Scissors
Split-eye needle

Instructions:
1 Working from the reel or a long strand of cord (this makes it more economical), thread about 2–3cm (¾–1¼in) of cord through the split-eye needle.

2 Thread the beads onto the cord in the desired pattern, starting with the focal bead. The number of beads used will be determined by the size of ring required.

3 Remove the needle, cut the cord at the required length and tie the two cord ends together using a double surgeon's knot (see page 7).

4 Pull the beads aside to expose the knot. Tug gently until the knot catches.

5 Re-thread the shorter tail through the needle and pass it through the focal bead (do not pull the knot into the bead yet). Remove the needle.

6 Coat the knot with clear nail polish to seal and secure.

7 Tug gently on the short tail until the knot pops into the focal bead.

8 Allow the nail polish to dry. Pull each cord gently away from the bead, taking care not to pull the knot back out of the bead, and snip the excess cord.

Add focus to a ring with a single bead that differs in shape or size or colour; adding spacer beads and/or bead caps can add emphasis to the focus. Using blue beads (above) gives a less dramatic effect.

Vintage-style Ring

Materials:
1 x 8 x 10mm purple faceted crystal rondelle
2 x 12mm bead caps
2 x 2.4mm round silver metal beads
Approx. 28–32 x 4 x 1.6mm daisy spacers
Stretchy cord
Clear nail polish

Tools:
Scissors
Split-eye needle

Instructions:

1 Working from the reel or a long strand of cord (this makes it more economical), thread about 2–3cm (¾–1¼in) of cord through the split-eye needle.

2 Thread the beads onto the cord in the desired pattern starting with a bead cap and ending with the larger crystal bead (this leaves the bead at one end and a bead cap at the other end of the cord). Thread a small metal bead on the outside of each bead cap to help hide the stretchy cord when transitioning to metal spacers at the curve. The number of daisy spacers used is determined by the size of ring required.

3 Remove the needle, cut the cord at the required length and tie the two cord ends together using a double surgeon's knot (see page 7).

4 Pull the beads aside to expose the knot. Tug gently until the knot catches.

5 Re-thread the shorter tail through the needle and pass it through the focal bead (do not pull the knot into the bead yet). Remove the needle.

6 Coat the knot with clear nail polish to seal and secure.

7 Tug gently on the short tail until the knot pops into the bead. It does not matter if the knot is too big to pass back into a bead, as it will be hidden within the bead cap.

8 Allow the nail polish to dry. Pull each cord gently away from the bead, taking care not to pull the knot back out of the bead, and snip the excess cord.

Use focus beads or metal beads of other colours to achieve different effects, as shown here.

Threading together lots of daisy spacers creates a very stylish ring that can alter its shape and size to fit any finger and maintain its gorgeous vintage finesse.

Double-stranded Ring

Materials:

Approx. 24–28 x 4 x 3mm rice-shaped
   freshwater pearls

1 x 8 x 10mm freshwater pearl as a focal bead

2 x 5mm diamante spacers

Stretchy cord

Clear nail polish

Tools:

Scissors

Split-eye needle

Instructions:

1 Working from the reel or a long strand of
cord (this makes it more economical), thread
about 2–3cm (¾–1¼in) of cord through the
split-eye needle.

2 Thread the beads onto the cord in the
desired pattern starting with a diamante spacer
and ending with the large freshwater pearl. The
number of rice-shaped pearls is determined by
the size of the ring required.

3 Remove the needle, cut the cord at the
required length and tie the two cord ends
together using a double surgeon's knot (see
page 7).

4 Pull the beads aside to expose the knot. Tug
gently until the knot catches.

5 Re-thread the shorter tail through the
needle and pass it through the focal bead (do
not pull the knot into the bead yet). Remove
the needle.

6 Coat the knot with clear nail polish to seal
and secure.

7 Tug gently on the short tail until the knot
pops into the bead. It does not matter if the
knot is too big to pass back into a bead, as it
will be hidden within the diamante spacer.

8 Allow the nail polish to dry. Pull each cord
gently away from the bead, taking care not to
pull the knot back out of the bead, and snip the
excess cord.

9 Repeat steps 1–8 with a second strand of
rice-shaped pearls, passing through the same
large freshwater pearl and diamante spacers.

*A double strand of beads for the
ring base is decorative as well as
adding substance. Use clear crystals
and gold spacers for a more sparkly
effect (see above).*

Diamante Spacer Bar Ring

Materials:

Approx. 32–36 x 3 x 4mm faceted crystal rondelles

3 x 12 x 2.5mm double-strand diamante spacer bars

Stretchy cord

Clear nail polish

Tools:

Scissors

Split-eye needle

Instructions:

1 Working from the reel or a long strand of cord (this makes it more economical), thread about 2–3cm (¾–1¼in) of cord through the split-eye needle.

2 Thread a diamante spacer bar then about 14–16 small crystal rondelles onto the cord (the number of crystal rondelles is determined by the size of the ring required). Add a second spacer bar, a small crystal rondelle, a third spacer bar and a final crystal rondelle. Ensure all the stones of the three spacer bars are facing the same direction.

3 Remove the needle, cut the cord at the required length and tie the two cord ends together using a double surgeon's knot (see page 7).

4 Pull the beads aside to expose the knot. Tug gently until the knot catches.

5 Re-thread the shorter tail through the needle and pass it through the focal bead (do not pull the knot into the bead yet). Remove the needle.

6 Coat the knot with clear nail polish to seal and secure.

7 Tug gently on the short tail until the knot pops into the bead. It does not matter if the knot is too big to pass back into a bead, as it will be hidden within the diamante spacer bar.

8 Allow the nail polish to dry. Pull each cord gently away from the bead, taking care not to pull the knot back out of the bead, and snip the excess cord.

9 Repeat steps 1–8 with a second strand of crystal rondelles, passing through the remaining hole of the diamante spacer bars.

Sparkling spacer bars capture double strands of glistening faceted crystals to create a stunning ring.

Fancy Spacer Bar Ring

Materials:

Approx. 30–36 x 4 x 3mm faceted crystal
rondelles

1 x 21 x 8mm fancy two-hole spacer bar

Stretchy cord

Clear nail polish

Tools:

Scissors

Split-eye needle

Instructions:

1 Working from the reel or a long strand of
cord (this makes it more economical), thread
about 2–3cm (¾–1¼in) of cord through the
split-eye needle.

2 Thread a diamante spacer bar onto the cord,
then about 15–18 small crystal rondelles (the
number of crystal rondelles is determined by
the size of the ring required).

3 Remove the needle, cut the cord at the
required length and tie the two cord ends
together using a double surgeon's knot (see
page 7).

4 Pull the beads aside to expose the knot. Tug
gently until the knot catches.

5 Re-thread the shorter tail through the
needle and pass it through the spacer bar (do
not pull the knot into the bead yet). Remove
the needle.

6 Coat the knot with clear nail polish to seal
and secure.

7 Tug gently on the short tail until the knot
pops into the spacer bar.

8 Allow the nail polish to dry. Pull each cord
gently away from the bead, taking care not to
pull the knot back out of the bead, and snip the
excess cord.

9 Repeat steps 1–8 with a second strand of
crystal rondelles, passing them through the
remaining hole of the diamante spacer bar.

*A single spacer bar or unusual shape can
create a very special and individual look
that is not only stunning, but also unique!*

Lavish Cha-cha Ring

Materials:

Approx. 14–16 x 3mm faceted round crystal AB (aurora borealis finish)

10 x 6mm faceted round crystal AB

10 x ball end head pins

Stretchy cord

Clear nail polish

Tools:

Scissors

Wire cutters

Round-nose pliers

Split-eye needle

Instructions:

1 Use the wire cutters to cut the ball end head pins to about 2cm (¾in) – enough to create two coil loops above a 6mm crystal bead.

2 Thread a 6mm facewted crystal onto a ball end head pin and make a coil loop with the round-nose pliers. Repeat with all the 6mm crystals (about 10).

3 Thread about 2–3cm (¾–1¼in) of cord through the split-eye needle, then pass it through about 14–16 of the 3mm crystals (the number of crystal rondelles is determined by the size of ring required).

4 Add the 6mm crystals by threading them through the coil loops.

5 Remove the needle and tie the two ends of the cord together using a double surgeon's knot (see page 7).

6 Pull the beads aside to expose the knot. Tug gently until the knot catches.

7 Coat the knot with clear nail polish to seal and secure.

8 Allow the nail polish to dry, then snip the excess cord. Pull the beads round to conceal the knot.

This ring gives off a timeless elegance with clusters of dazzling crystals on a band of yet more glistening crystals! Alternatively, use grey pearls for a more subtle look (see above).

Precious Flower Ring

Materials:

0.8mm wire

Tools:

Ring mandrel
Wire cutters
Chain-nose pliers
Nylon-jaw pliers

Instructions:

1 Lay the ring mandrel in the middle of a 35–40cm (13¾–15¾in) length of wire. Wrap the left side of the wire round the ring mandrel, then repeat with the right side of the wire. The wire should be lying side by side at a position one size larger than the desired finished ring size. Bring the wire together at the front where you started. This will give you three strands of wire round the back of the mandrel.

2 Bring the wires together and twist them round each other once to hold the chosen size and create the 'centre' of the flower. Use the nylon-jaw pliers to smooth out the wire if it gets bent or kinked at any point.

3 Wrap one wire until it lies alongside the other and wrap both wires together or one at a time, round that first twist. Continue until you have the size of bud or flower desired or until you have 3–4cm (1¼–1½in) of wire remaining at the end of each wire tail.

4 Bring one wire to the right of the flower with the other remaining on the left.

5 Remove the ring from the mandrel and use chain-nose pliers to wrap the wire tails round the body of the ring, close to the flower. Wrap two to three tight, neat loops on either side of the flower.

6 Cut the excess wire and tuck the ends away so they do not scratch.

7 Replace the ring on the mandrel to shape it.

By chasing wire round the central wrap, you can create an exquisitely organic floral bud. Variations can be created with the use of gold seed beads in the centre (see opposite).

Duet Ring

Materials:

0.8mm wire

2 x purple jasper beads or turquoise beads

Tools:

Ring mandrel

Wire cutters

Chain-nose pliers

Nylon-jaw pliers

Instructions:

1 Lay the ring mandrel in the middle of a 35–40cm (13¾–15¾in) length of wire. Wrap the left side of the wire round the ring mandrel, then repeat with the right side of the wire. The wire should be lying side by side at a position one size larger than the desired finished ring size. Bring the wire together at the front where you started. This will give you three strands of wire round the back of the mandrel.

2 Bring the wires together and twist them round each other once or twice to hold the chosen ring size. Use the nylon-jaw pliers to smooth out the wire if it gets bent or kinked at any point.

3 Add a bead to one tail of wire. Push the bead to the central twist and wrap the wire round the bead as many times as desired,

leaving at least 3cm (1¼in) of wire. Repeat with the second bead on the other tail of wire.

4 Bring one wire tail to the right of the beads with the remaining wire to the left.

5 Remove the ring from the mandrel and use chain-nose pliers to wrap the wire tails round the body of the ring (three strands from step 1) close to the beads. Wrap two or three tight, neat loops then repeat on the other side.

6 Cut the excess the wire and tuck the ends away so they do not scratch.

7 Replace the ring on the mandrel to shape it.

Using a front wrap and two beautiful beads, you can create a stylish ring to coordinate with or accent any outfit.

Fabulous Cluster Ring

Materials:

0.8mm wire

2 x 8mm faceted crystals

2 x 6mm glass pearls

Tools:

Ring mandrel

Wire cutters

Chain-nose pliers

Nylon-jaw pliers

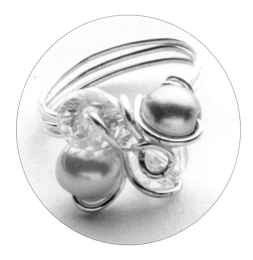

Instructions:

1 Lay the ring mandrel in the middle of a 40–45cm (15¾–17¾in) length of wire. Wrap the left side of the wire round the ring mandrel, then repeat with the right side of the wire. The wire should be lying side by side at a position one size larger than the desired finished ring size. Bring the wire together at the front where you started. This will give you three strands of wire round the back of the mandrel.

2 Bring wires together and twist round each other one or two times to hold the chosen ring size. Use the nylon-jaw pliers to smooth out the wire if it gets bent or kinked at any point.

3 Add a bead to one tail of wire and wrap the wire round the bead if desired. Now add a second bead and wrap it similarly, positioning it at a right angle to the first bead.

4 Repeat step 3 with the other the tail of wire. When finished, the four beads will form a tight square. Ensure there is at least 3cm (1¼in) of

wire remaining on each wire tail. Bring one wire tail to the right of the beads leaving the other on the left.

5 Remove the ring from the mandrel and use chain-nose pliers to wrap the wire tails round the body of ring, close to the beads. Wrap two tight, neat loops, then repeat on the other side.

6 Cut the excess wire and tuck the ends away so they do not scratch.

7 Replace the ring on the mandrel to shape it.

With several beads and flourishes of wire, you can create unique, eye-catching rings.

Extravagant Cluster Ring

Materials:

0.8mm wire

A mix of 4mm and 6mm bicone beads in crystal, jet and red

Tools:

Ring mandrel

Wire cutters

Chain-nose pliers

Nylon-jaw pliers

Instructions:

1 Lay the ring mandrel in the middle of a 50–55cm (19¾–21¾in) length of wire. Wrap the left side of the wire round the ring mandrel, then repeat with the right side of the wire. The wire should be lying side by side at a position one size larger than the desired finished ring size. Bring the wire together at the front where you started. This will give you three strands of wire round the back of the mandrel.

2 Bring the wires together and twist them round each other one or two times to hold the chosen ring size. Use the nylon-jaw pliers to smooth out the wire if it gets bent or kinked at any point.

3 Add a bead to one tail of wire and wrap the wire round the bead if desired. Now add a second bead, wrap it similarly and position it.

4 Repeat step 3 with the other tail of wire. Continue adding beads back and forth between the two tails until you have a cluster

that appeals. Add wire loops and flourishes as desired. Ensure there is at least 3cm (1¼in) of wire remaining on each wire tail. Bring one wire tail to the right of the beads leaving the other on the left.

5 Remove the ring from the mandrel and use chain-nose pliers to wrap the wire tails round the body of the ring, close to the beads. Wrap two to three tight, neat loops, then repeat on other side.

6 Cut the excess wire and tuck the ends away so they do not scratch.

7 Replace the ring on the mandrel to shape it.

Clusters of beads in
coordinating colours enhanced
with wire loops and flourishes
can look very opulent.

Solitaire Ring

Materials:

0.8mm wire

1 x faceted bead

Tools:

Ring mandrel

Wire cutters

Chain-nose pliers

Nylon-jaw pliers

Instructions:

1 Thread the bead to the centre of a 40cm (15¾in) length of wire. Place the bead against a ring mandrel, about one size larger than the desired finished size. Wrap both tails round to the back of the mandrel, then back to the front. This gives you two strands of wire round the back of the mandrel.

2 Hold each wire tail and twist them at the same time round the bead while the bead and wire are correctly placed on the ring mandrel.

3 Continue to wrap round the bead until you like the look, ensuring that there is still 3cm (1¼in) of wire remaining on each wire tail. Use the nylon-jaw pliers to smooth out the wire if it gets bent or kinked at any point.

4 Bring one wire tail to the right of the bead, leaving the other strand of wire on the left.

5 Remove the ring from the mandrel and use chain-nose pliers to wrap the wire tails round the body of the ring, close to the beads. Wrap two to three tight, neat loops, then repeat on the other side.

6 Cut the excess wire and tuck the ends away so they do not scratch.

7 Replace the ring on the mandrel to shape it.

The beauty of a solitaire ring focuses on the single bead, enhanced by the silver wire frame surrounding it.

Fancy Solitaire Ring

Materials:
0.8mm wire

1 x large, flat bead

Tools:
Ring mandrel

Wire cutters

Chain-nose pliers

Nylon-jaw pliers

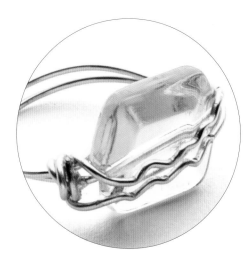

Instructions:

1 Thread a bead to the centre of a 40cm (15¾in) length of wire. Place the bead against a ring mandrel, about one size larger than the desired finished size. Wrap both tails round to back of mandrel then back to the front. This gives you two strands of wire round the back of the mandrel.

2 Hold each wire tail and twist them at the same time round the bead while the bead and wire are correctly placed on the ring mandrel.

3 Run one strand across the top or front of the bead. Run the other strand across the bottom or back of the bead so that the two strands finish on opposite sides of the bead. Ensure there is still 6–8cm (2½–3¼in) of wire remaining on each wire tail. Use the nylon-jaw pliers to smooth out the wire if it gets bent or kinked at any point.

4 Bring one wire tail to the right of the bead, leaving the other on the left.

5 Remove the ring from the mandrel and use chain-nose pliers to wrap the wire tails round the body of the ring, close to the bead. Wrap several tight, neat loops then repeat on the other side.

6 Use the chain-nose pliers to create kinks or waves in the wire across the top of the bead.

7 Cut the excess wire and tuck the ends away so they do not scratch.

8 Replace the ring on the mandrel to shape it.

Wire flourishes add to the character and interest of the chosen bead.

Swirled Multi-strand Ring

Materials:

0.8mm wire

6 x 6mm round, faceted crystals AB (aurora borealis finish)

Tools:

Ring mandrel

Wire cutters

Chain-nose pliers

Nylon-jaw pliers

Instructions:

1 Lay the ring mandrel in the middle of three 20–30cm (7¾–11¾in) lengths of wire. Wrap the three strands on the left round to the front of the mandrel, then repeat with strands on the right. The wire should be lying side by side at a position one size larger than the desired finished ring size. Bring the wires together at the front where you started. This will give you three strands of wire round the back of the mandrel.

2 Bring the wires together and twist them completely round each other once to hold the chosen ring size.

3 Holding the mandrel up, have the top three wires pointing down and the bottom three wires pointing up.

4 Take the right wire pointing up and thread a bead down to the twist of the wires. Bend that wire to the right, then remove the ring from the mandrel and, with chain-nose pliers, wrap the wire tail twice round the ring base as close to the bead as possible. Trim the excess wire and tuck in the ends. Use the nylon-jaw pliers to smooth out the wire if it gets bent or kinked at any point.

5 Return the ring to the mandrel. Take the middle wire pointing up and thread a bead

down to the twist of wires. Bend that wire to the right, following the line of the previous bead (step 4). Remove the ring from the mandrel and with chain-nose pliers, wrap the wire tail twice round the ring base right next to the wire wraps from step 4. Trim the excess wire and tuck in the ends.

6 Return the ring to the mandrel. Take the left wire pointing up and thread a bead down to the twist of wires. Bend that wire to the right, following the line of the previous bead (step 5). Remove the ring from the mandrel and, using chain-nose pliers, wrap the wire tail twice round the ring base right next to the wire wraps from step 5. Then trim the excess wire and tuck in the ends.

7 Return the ring to the mandrel, but turn it round so the remaining three wires are pointing up. Repeat steps 4 to 6 to complete the ring.

8 Replace the ring on the mandrel to shape it.

Use multiple strands of wire to create striking swirls with glistening crystal beads. The AB, or aurora borealis finish on these beads gives a sparkling rainbow effect.

Beaded Ring with Coils

Materials:

0.8mm wire

2 x 12mm oval
faceted crystals

Tools:

Ring mandrel

Wire cutters

Chain-nose pliers

Nylon-jaw pliers

Round-nose pliers

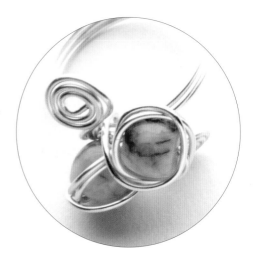

Instructions:

1 Lay the ring mandrel in the middle of three 30–40cm (11¾–15¾in) lengths of wire, wrap the three strands on the left round to the front of the ring mandrel, then repeat with the strands on the right. The wire should be lying side by side at a position one size larger than the desired finished ring size. Bring the wire together at the front where you started. This will give you three strands of wire round the back of the mandrel.

2 Bring the wires together and twist them round each other once to hold the chosen ring size.

3 Add a bead to a strand of wire on the left of the ring centre. Wrap with the wire and place it vertically, then secure it using chain-nose pliers to wrap the wire tail round the left side of the ring base two times, tight and close to the bead. Do not trim but bring it up to the front of the ring ready for step 4. Repeat with another bead on the right side of the ring centre. Use the nylon-jaw pliers to smooth out the wire if it gets bent or kinked at any point.

4 Trim three tails of wire so you have one 6cm (2½in) and one 4.5cm (1¾in) tail on each side.

5 Using the round-nose pliers, form coils. Arrange the coils on either side of the vertical beads.

6 Replace the ring on the mandrel to shape it.

Wire coils are a great way to embellish and add a touch of whimsy to wire rings.

Chain Stitch Beaded Ring

Materials:

Approx. 48 size 8/0 E
beads

Approx. 180 size 11/0
seed beads

WildFire thread

Tools:

Scissors

Split-eye needle

Instructions:

1 Thread 2–3cm (¾–1¼in) of a 2m (2¼yd) strand of WildFire thread through a split-eye needle. Referring to diagram 1, pick up six E beads and, leaving a tail of about 10cm (4in), pass the needle and thread through the beads again, and line them so that they are stacked and lying with a chain of three beads next to another chain of three beads. Pull out any slack thread.

2 Create a third chain by adding three more E beads to the thread, then pass the needle back through the previous chain of three E beads placed in step 1 (start from the opposite end from where the needle and thread exited

on the last layer of three beads), and pass the needle back through the new chain of E beads. Pull out any slack so the beads lie close and neat, next to each other. Continue until the chains of beads reach the desired length.

3 Join the two ends by threading twice through and round the first and last bead chains.

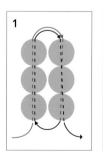

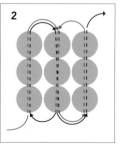

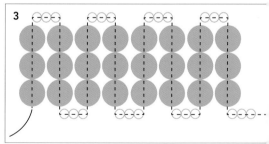

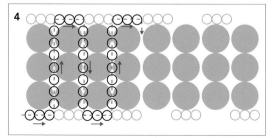

38

4 Referring to diagram 3, pick up three seed beads and pass the needle through the closest chain of beads. At the other side, add another three seed beads and pass through the next chain of beads. Continue adding three seed beads between chains of beads on either side of the ring until the seed beads are continuous on either exposed edge of E bead chains.

5 Pass through one seed bead so that the thread is now positioned between two chains of E beads. Referring to diagram 4, pick up seven seed beads (or whatever number is necessary to create a continuous line of beads), and lay them along the groove between E bead chains. Pass the needle through three seed beads along the opposite edge. Create another line of seven seed beads to lie in the next groove between seed bead chains. Continue until you have covered all the grooves. Weave both thread ends through the beads to secure and trim the excess.

Seed bead stripes give another dimension when added over large, shiny E beads.

Flat-stitched Lacy Ring

Materials:

Approx. 170 size 11/0 seed beads
   in silver and black

WildFire thread

Tools:

Scissors

Split-eye needle

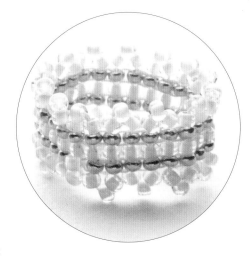

Instructions:

1 Thread 2–3cm (¾–1¼in) of a 2m (2¼yd) strand of WildFire thread through a split-eye needle. Add a stop bead about 10cm (4in) from the end of the thread.

2 Referring to diagram 1 below, start at 'a', pick up a single colour 1 (silver) seed bead, a single colour 2 (black) seed bead and then a single colour 1 seed bead.

3 Pick up a colour 1 seed bead and sew back through the last seed bead (colour 1) of the first row and through the colour 1 seed bead added at the beginning of this step, bringing you to 'b'.

4 Pick up a colour 2 seed bead and sew back through the middle seed bead (colour 2) of the first row, and through the colour 2 seed bead at the beginning of this step.

5 Pick up a colour 1 seed bead and sew back through the remaining seed bead (colour 1) of the first row, and through the colour 1 seed bead added at the beginning of this step, bringing you to 'c'.

6 Continue stitching a new row as in steps 2–5 above until you reach the required size and an even number of rows.

7 Create a ring by joining the ends in the same way as adding a new row.

8 To create the lacy edge, refer to diagram 2. At 'a', pick up three colour 1 seed beads and pass the needle down though the closest row of seed beads of the ring, bringing you to 'b'. Pick up another three seed beads and pass the needle up through the next row of seed beads of the ring, bringing you to 'c'.

9 Continue in this way until you have added lacy edges to all the beads, then weave both thread ends back through the beads to secure and trim the excess.

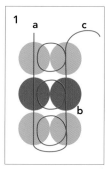

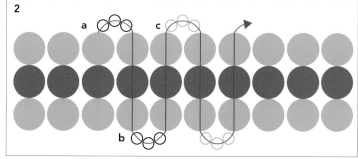

Adding triplets of seed beads along the edge of a woven ring creates a delicate, almost like-lace look.

Right-angle Weave Band

Materials:
Approx. 100 x black or silver seed beads
10–12 x 4 x 3mm crystal rondelles
WildFire thread

Tools:
Scissors
Split-eye needle

Instructions:

1 Thread 2–3cm (¾–1¼in) of a 2m (2¼yd) strand of WildFire thread through a split-eye needle. Referring to diagram 1, pick up a crystal rondelle, three seed beads, a second crystal rondelle and three seed beads. Pass the thread back through the first crystal rondelle, the next three seed beads and the second crystal rondelle to form a circle.

2 Referring to diagram 2, pick up three seed beads, a crystal rondelle and three seed beads. Pass the thread back through the crystal rondelle from the previous circle of beads. Continue through the first three seed beads and crystal rondelle added at the beginning of this step, to form a new circle of beads.

3 Repeat step 2 until the ring is three seed beads less than the desired size.

4 To join the ring ends, starting from the last rondelle, pick up three seed beads, pass through the rondelle from the other end of the ring, add three seed beads and then back through the first rondelle from the beginning of this step.

5 As an optional step, thread round once more, adding a seed bead to the top of each rondelle. This will make the line of seed beads continuous, as in the ring opposite. Alternatively, you could omit this step to achieve the finish in the photograph above.

6 Weave both thread ends back through the beads to secure and trim the excess thread.

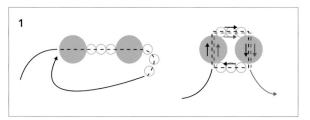

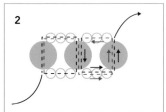

The matt black seed beads complement the mirror surface of the silver faceted rondelle beads to create this wonderfully sophisticated ring.

Right-angle Weave Focus

Materials:

Approx. 80 x gold seed beads

6 x 4mm black bicone crystals

1 x freshwater pearl

WildFire thread

Tools:

Scissors

Split-eye needle

Instructions:

1 Thread 2–3cm (¾–1¼in) of a 2m (2¼yd) strand of WildFire thread through a split-eye needle. Referring to the diagram below (working from the left), pick up the freshwater pearl, a seed bead and three bicone crystals, each with a seed bead after it. Sew into a circle leaving a tail of about 10cm (4in). Continue sewing round the circle through the freshwater pearl, seed bead, bicone, seed bead and bicone.

2 Pick up six seed beads and stitch a circle round and back through the bicone crystal, at 'a', where the thread exited in step 1. Pass the needle through the first four seed beads from the beginning of this step.

3 Pick up six seed beads and stitch a circle round and back through the third and fourth seed beads from step 2, as 'b'. Pass the needle through the first four seed beads from the beginning of this step.

4 Continue stitching circles of seed beads (as in step 3) until about 1cm (½in) before reaching the desired length for the ring.

5 Pick up two seed beads, a bicone crystal and two seed beads. Sew a circle back through the third and fourth seed beads (central two seed beads) from the last circle of seed beads. Pass the needle through the first two seed beads and the bicone crystal from the beginning of this step.

6 Pick up a seed bead, a bicone crystal and a seed bead, then pass the needle through the freshwater pearl from step 1; add a seed bead, a bicone crystal and a seed bead. Sew through the bicone from step 5. Stitch round again, then weave the thread back through the beads to secure. Cut away the excess. Weave the other end of the thread through the beads to secure and cut away the excess.

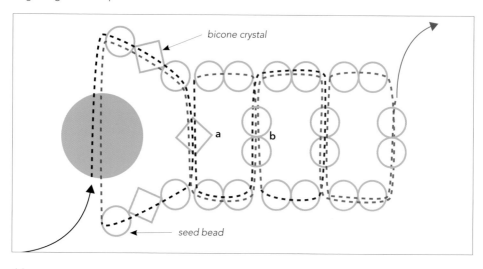

bicone crystal

a   b

seed bead

Use the contrast of jet bicones and antique gold seed beads to embellish an exquisite freshwater pearl.

Ring of Daisies

Materials:

Approx. 120 size 11/0 black
  seed beads

5–6 x 4mm crystal bicones
  in each of two colours

WildFire thread

Tools:

Scissors

Split-eye needle

Note: for this project, follow the technique on page 7 for 'How to make a daisy chain'.

Instructions:

1 Thread 2–3cm (¾–1¼in) of a 2m (2¼yd) strand of WildFire thread through a split-eye needle. Pick up 12 seed beads and sew a circle by passing back through the first three seed beads added. Pull tight.

2 Pick up a crystal in colour 1 and count six seed beads from where the thread exits the seed bead from step 1.

3 Pass the needle through the sixth seed bead from the opposite direction, that is, from the side where it touches the seventh seed bead through the sixth seed bead, the fifth seed bead and the fourth, exiting between the third and fourth seed beads.

4 Pick up nine seed beads and sew a circle by passing back through the last three seed beads in the previous step (the sixth, then the fifth, then the fourth).

5 Pick up a crystal in colour 2 and count six seed beads from where the thread exited the seed bead from the previous step. Pass the needle through the sixth seed bead from the

opposite direction, that is, from the side where it touches the seventh seed bead through the sixth seed bead, the fifth seed bead and the fourth, exiting between the third and fourth seed beads.

6 Repeat steps 4 and 5 until you have reached 5–6mm (³/₁₆–¼in) short of the desired size of your ring.

7 Pick up three seed beads and pass the needle through the corresponding three seed beads from the ring of seed beads at the other end of the ring (beads 4, 5 and 6). Pick up three seed beads and complete the circle by passing the needle through three seed beads. Add the crystal as before.

8 Weave both ends of thread through the beads to secure and cut away the excess.

The repeating pattern of glistening crystals circled with seed beads creates a chain that is both classic and stylish.

Acknowledgements

I would like to thank the team at Search Press for their patience and support, particularly May Corfield and Angela Baynham for editorial support, Fiona Murray for styling and the gorgeous photography (rings are really hard to photograph), and to Marrianne Miall for her design work and turning my scribbles into clear and helpful diagrams. A very special mention must go to Beadalon, whose products I always use and recommend to my students due to their unrivalled quality. I thank them for supporting me with tools and materials for this and all my books on jewellery and beading! Of course, a huge thank you to everyone who has purchased a copy of this book – it is my sincere hope that it will inspire and bring much pleasure to all!

Publisher's Note
You are invited to visit the author's website:
www.carolynschulz.com